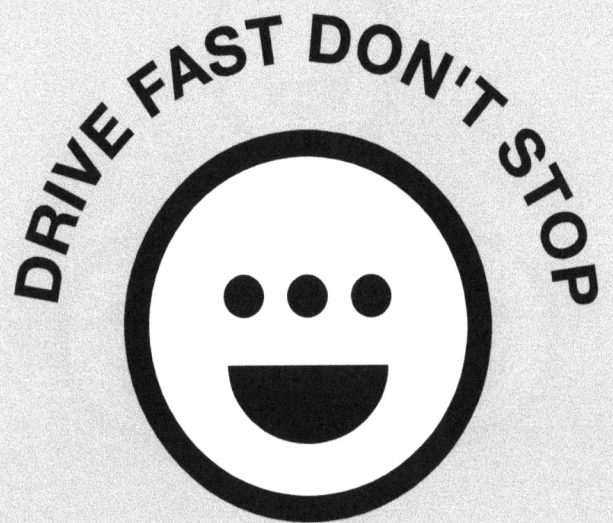

DRIVE FAST DON'T STOP

3

DRIVE FAST DON'T STOP

BOOK THREE

VOLKSWAGEN
TOYOTA

FAST DON'T

FAST DON'T

E FAST DON'T S

VE FAST DON'T ST

RIVE FAST DON'T STO

DRIVE FAST DON'T STOP

DRIVE FAST DON'T STOP

DRIVE FAST DON'T STOP

VOLKSWAGEN

VOLKSWAGEN

VOLKSWAGEN

VOLKSWAGEN

VOLKSWAGEN

VOLKSWAGEN

VOLKSWAGEN

VOLKSWAGEN

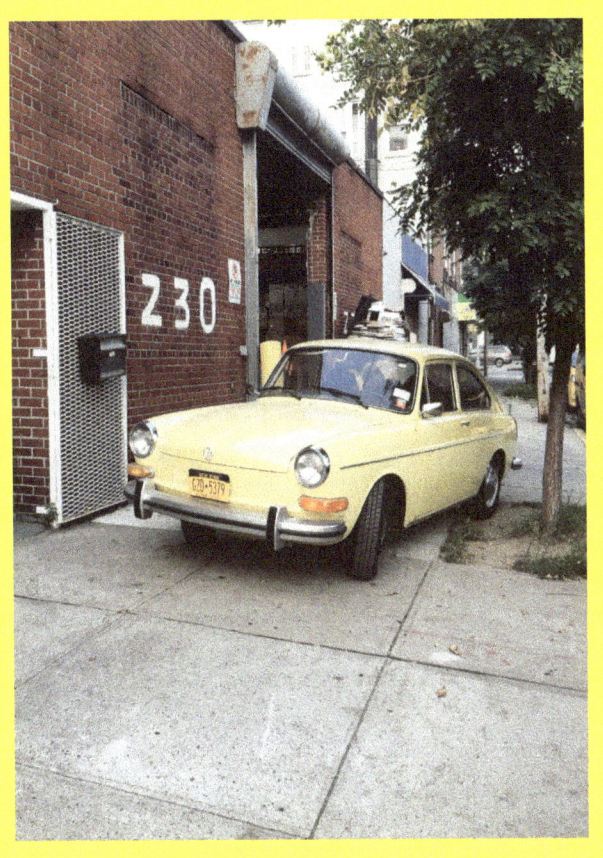

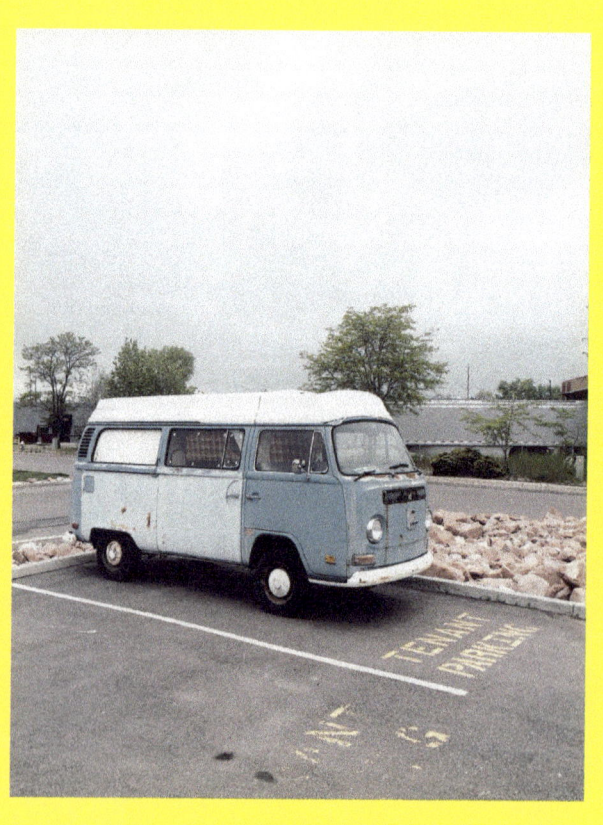

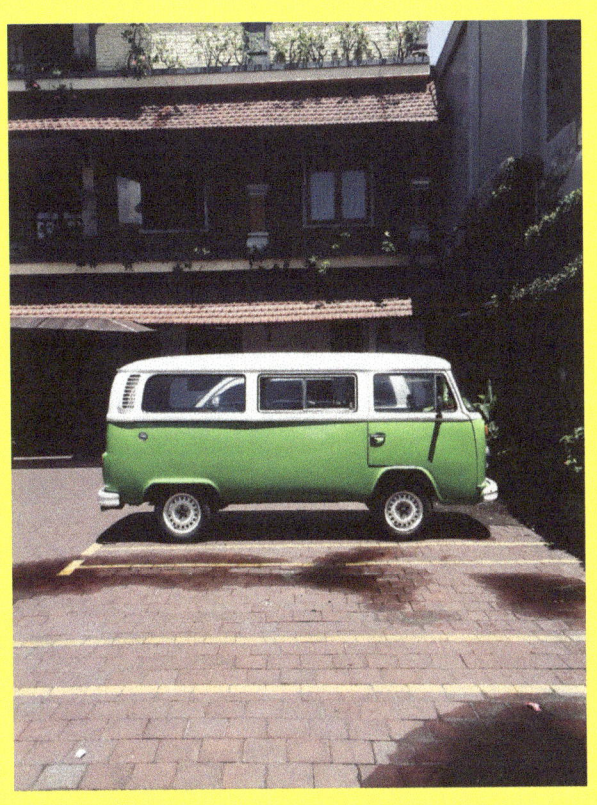

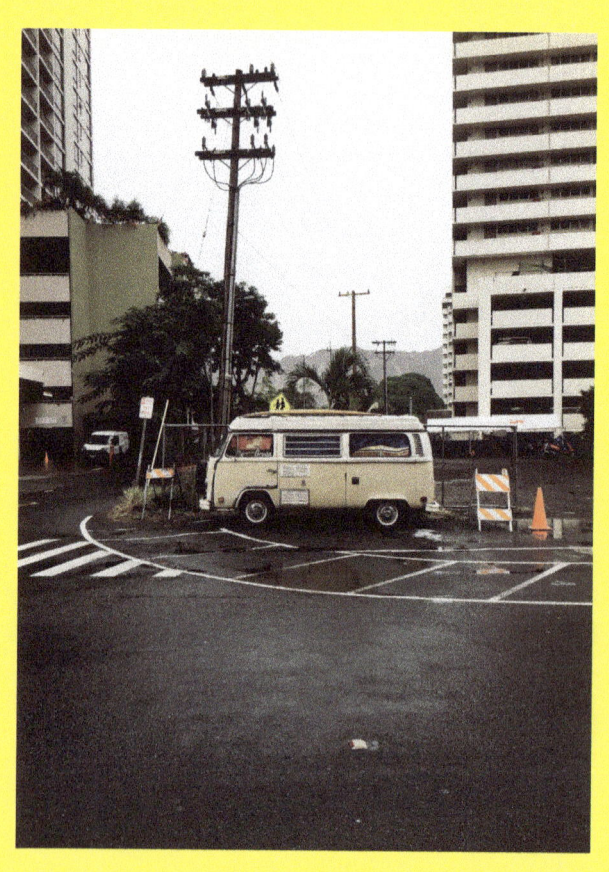

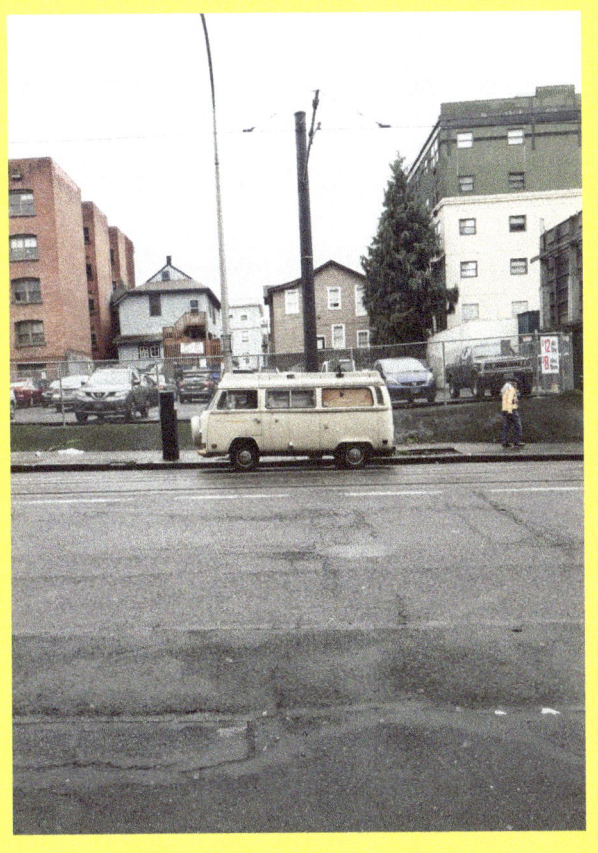

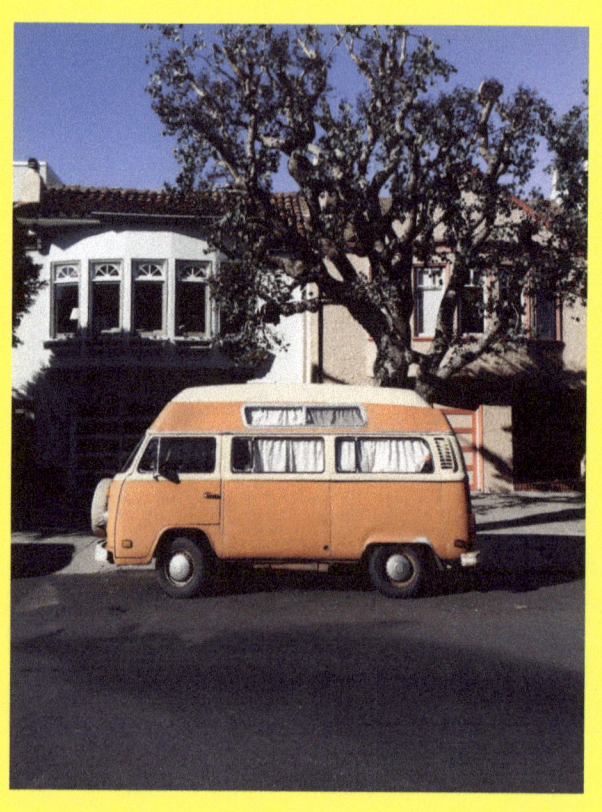

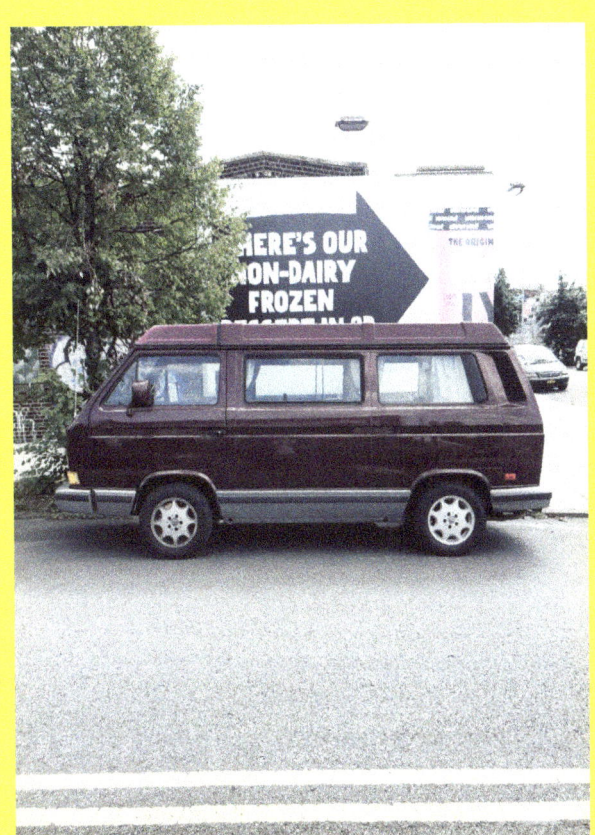

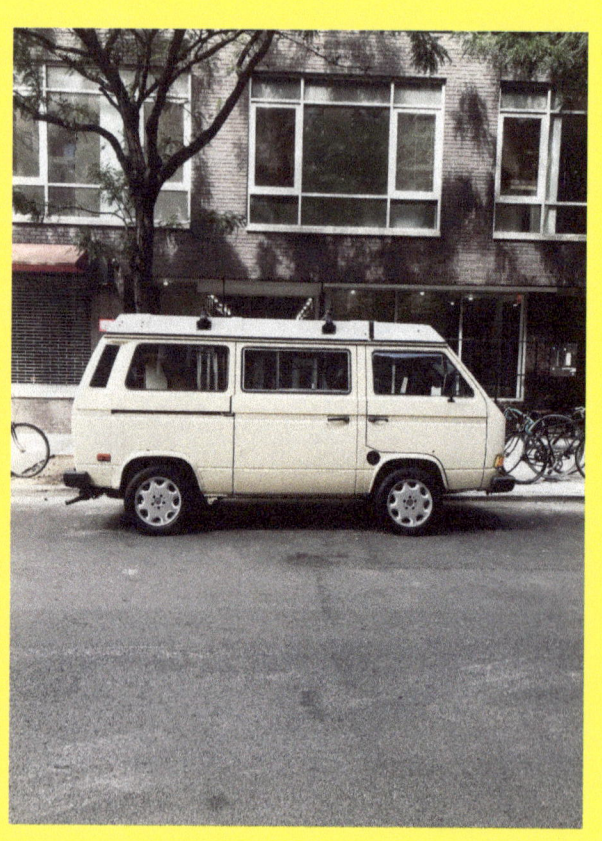

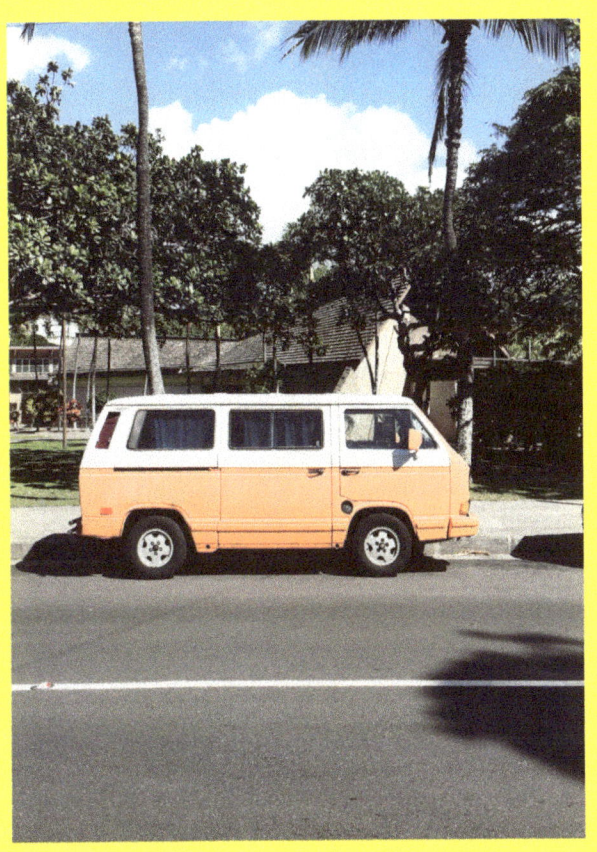

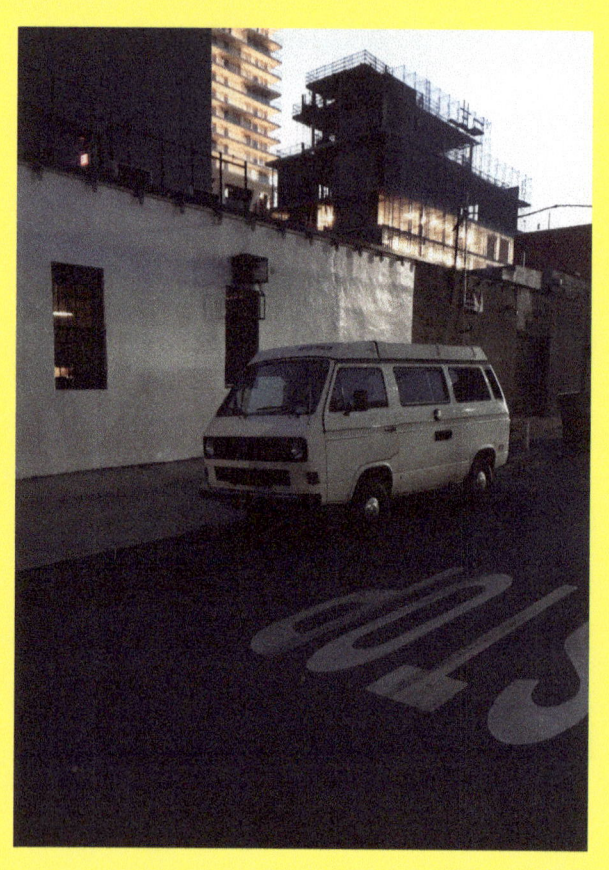

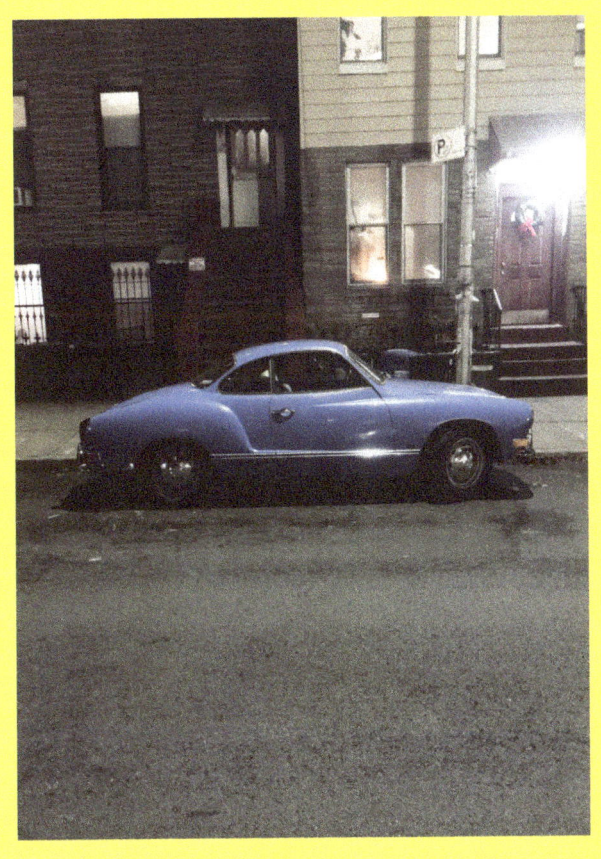

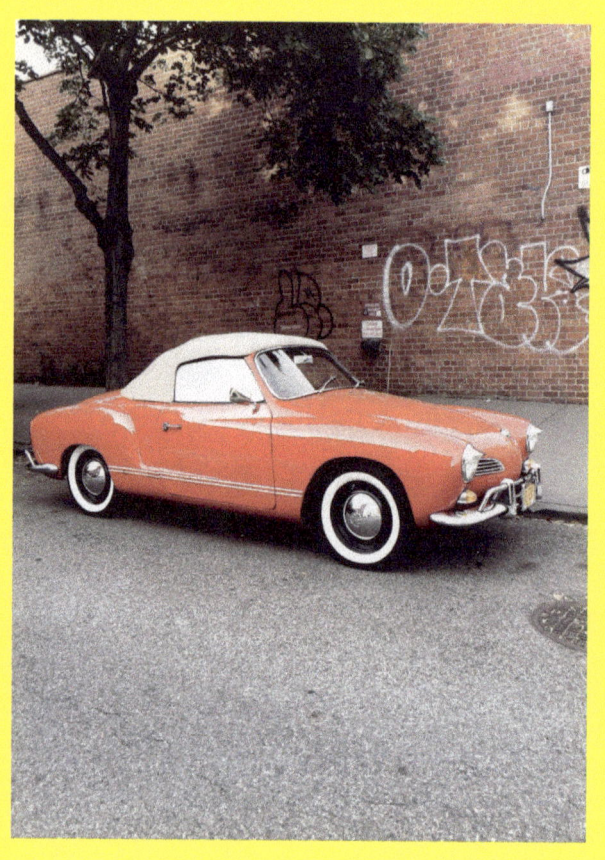

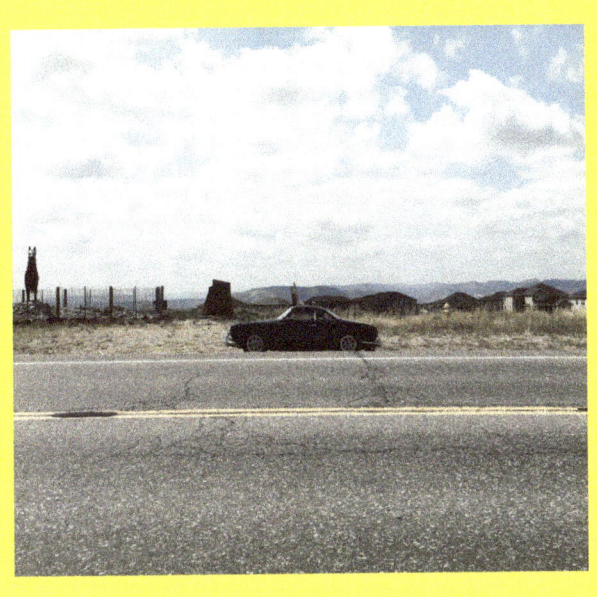

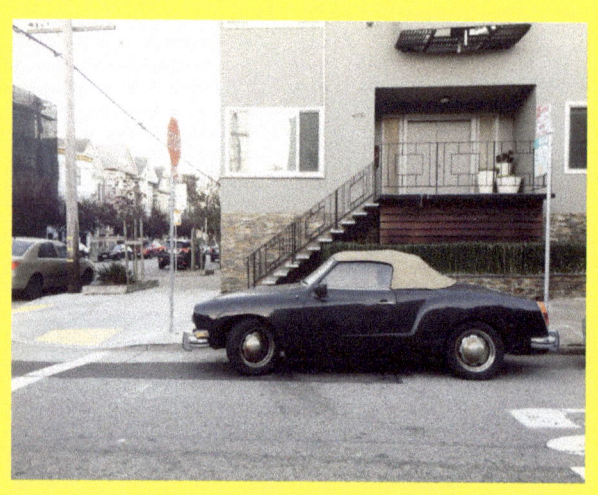

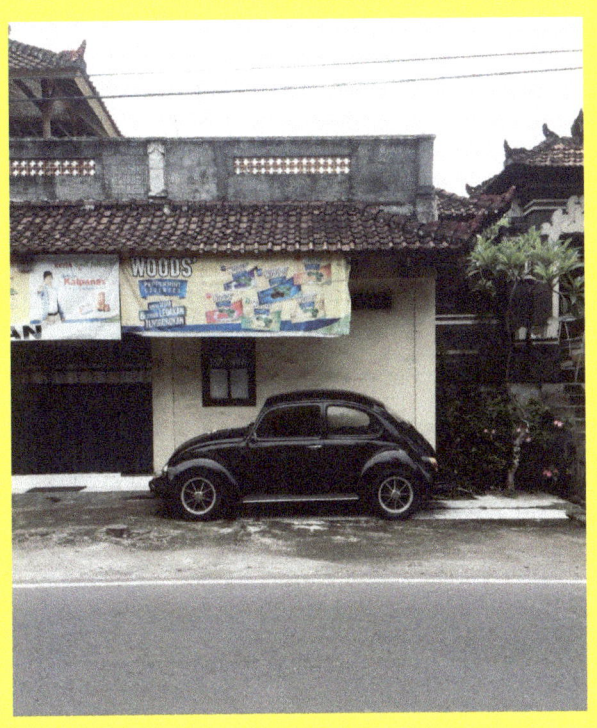

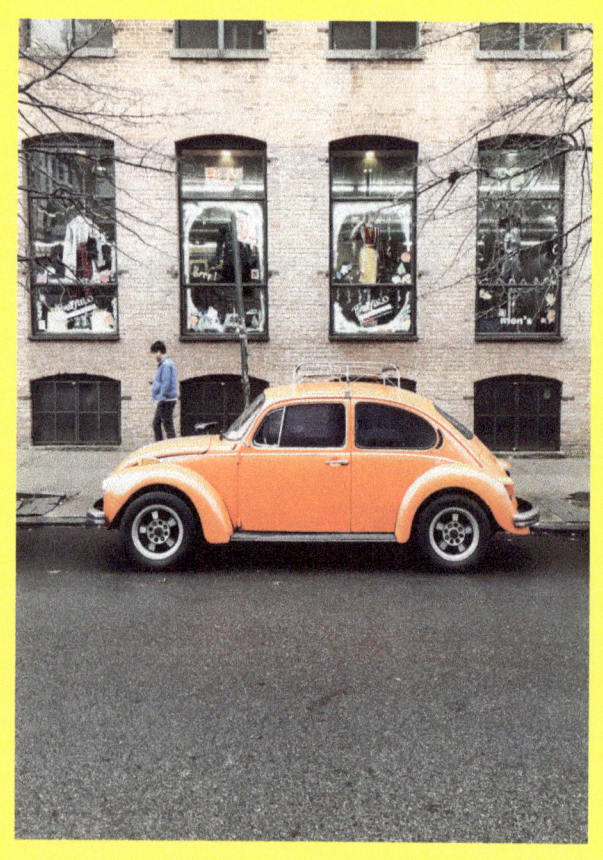

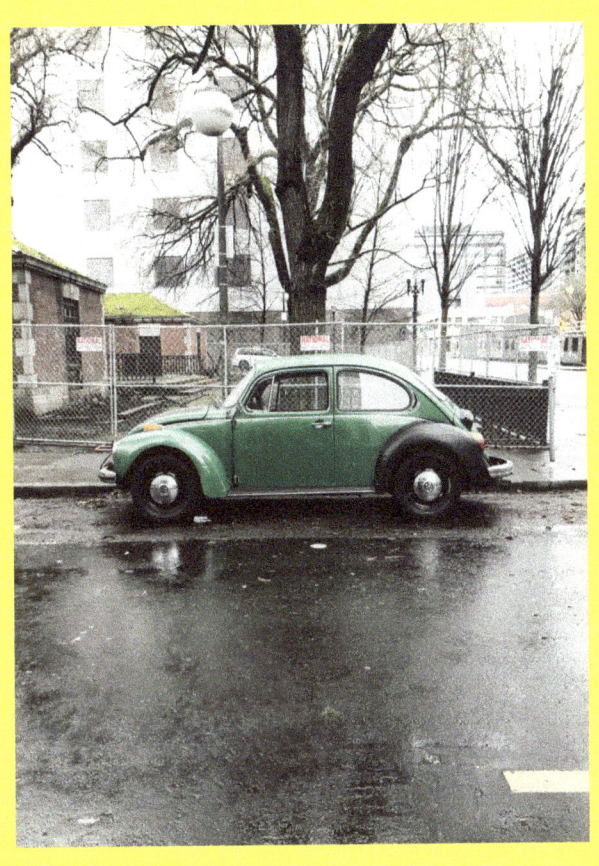

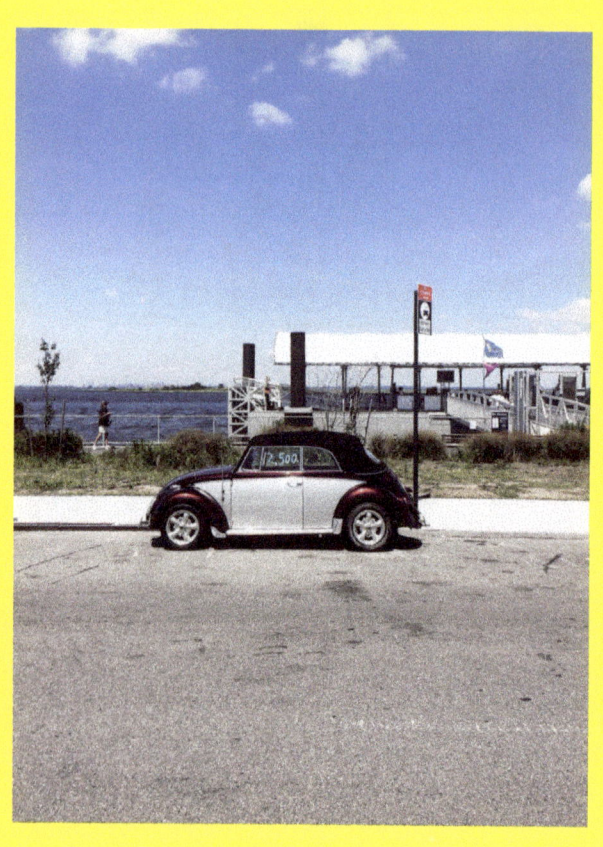

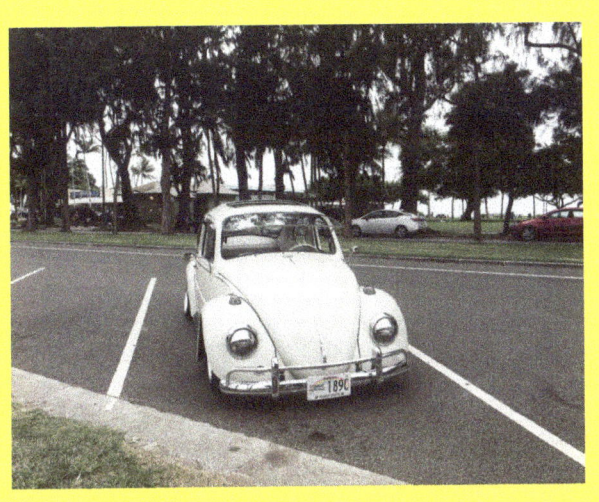

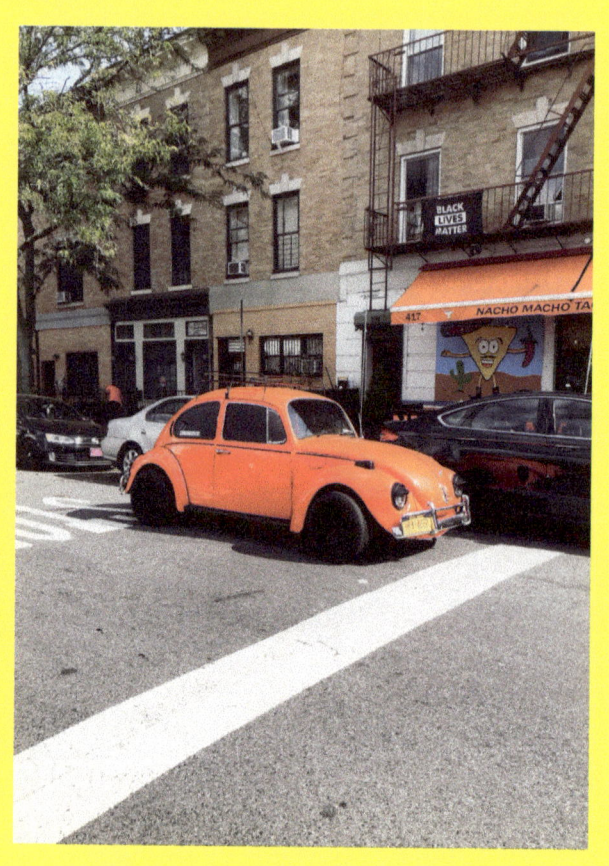

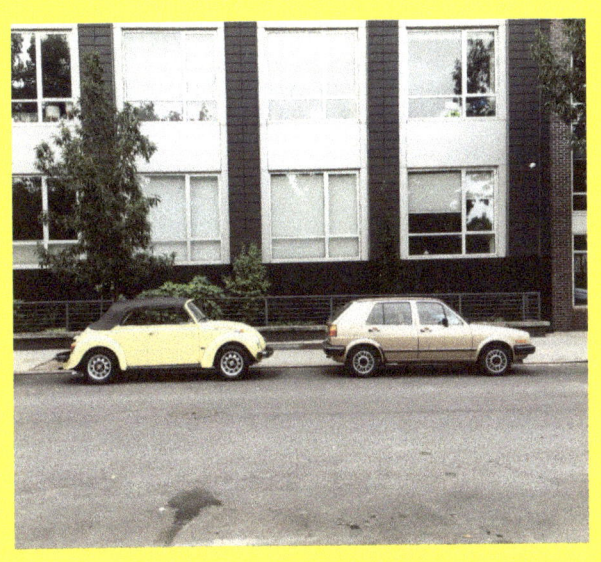

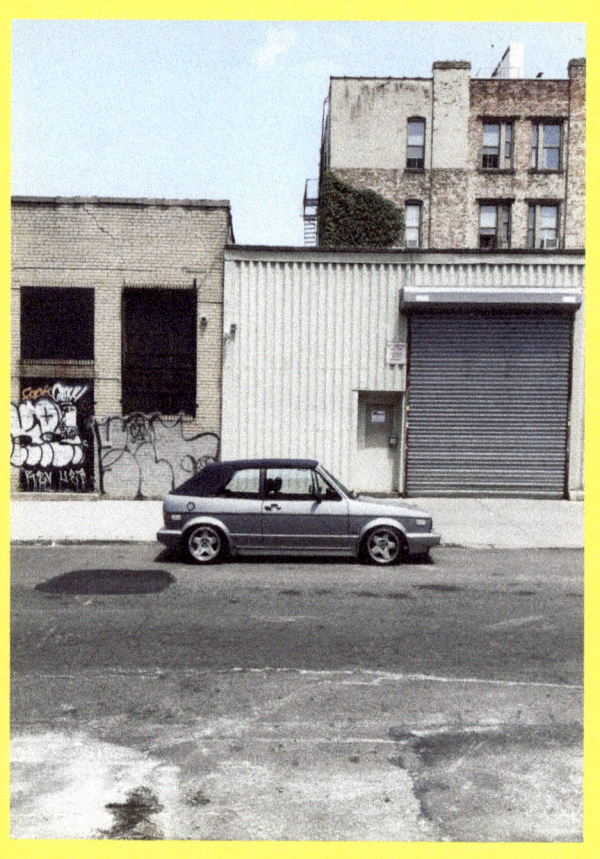

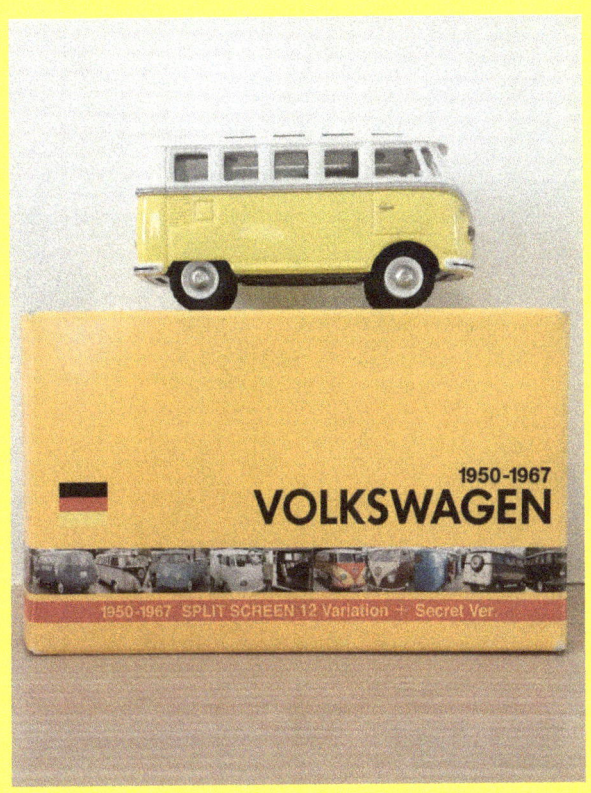

TOYOTA

TOYOTA

TOYOTA

TOYOTA

TOYOTA

TOYOTA

TOYOTA

TOYOTA

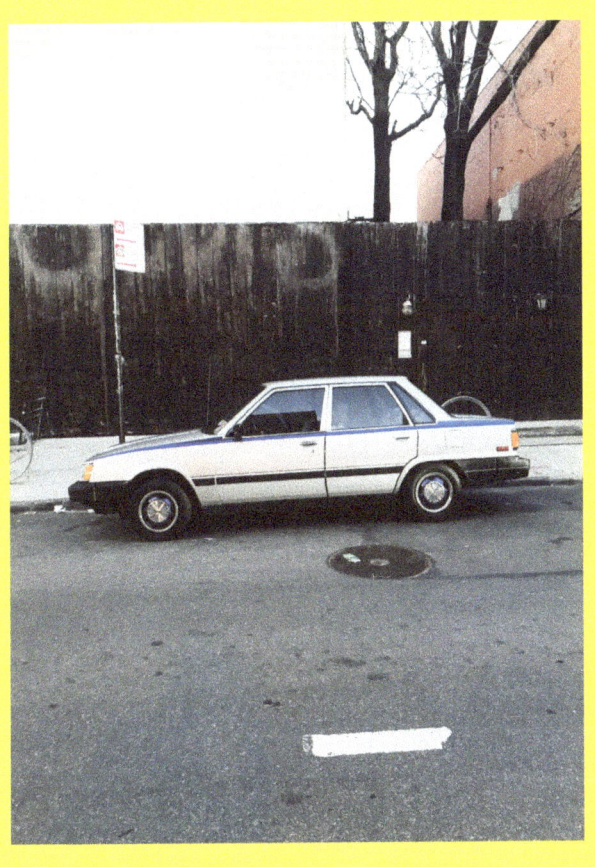

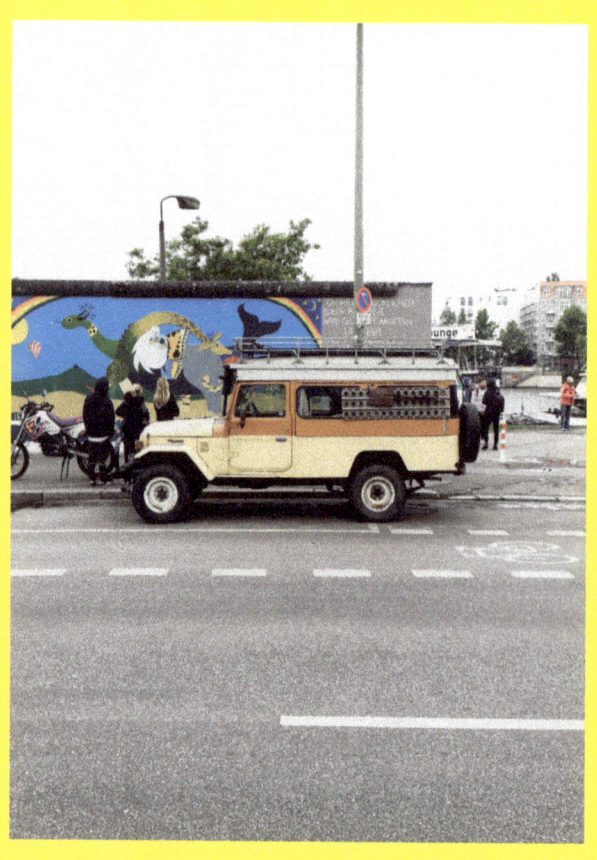

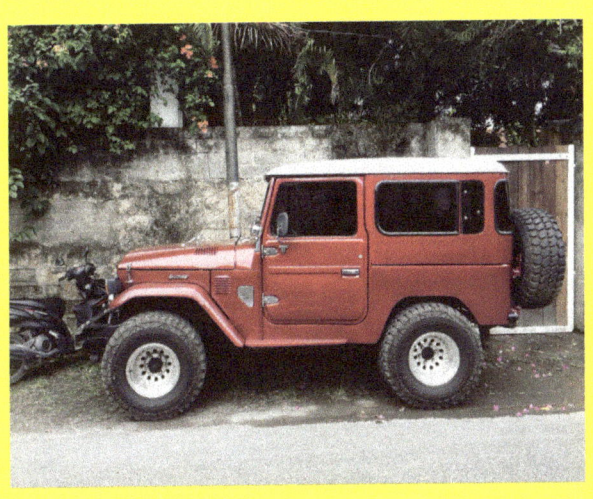

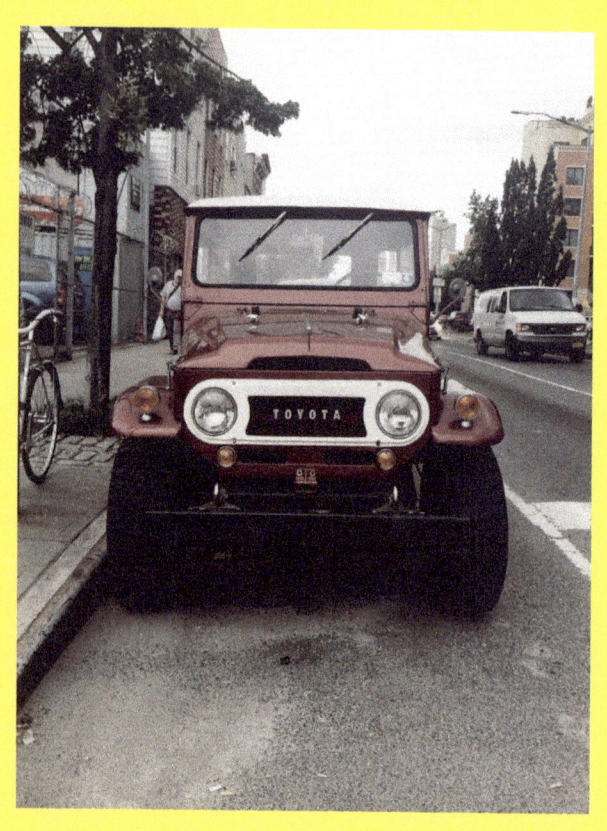

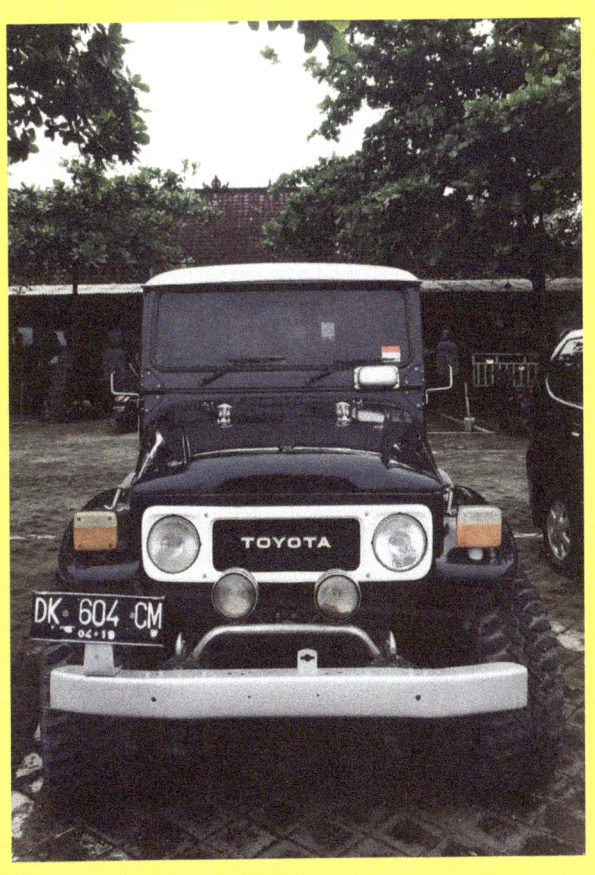

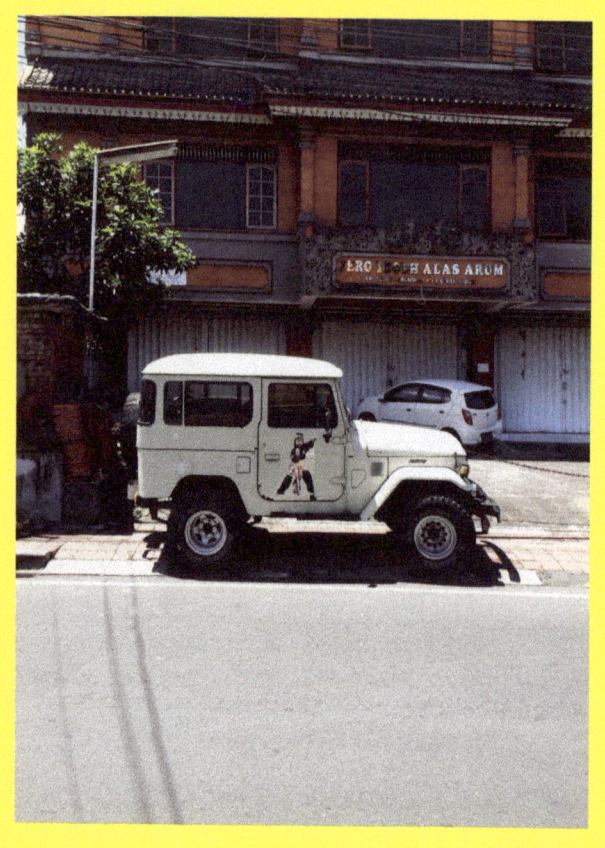

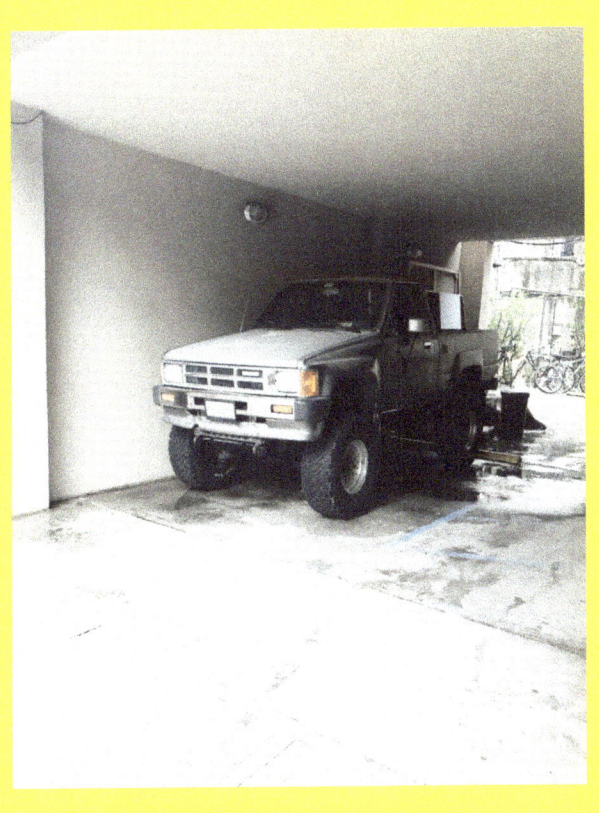

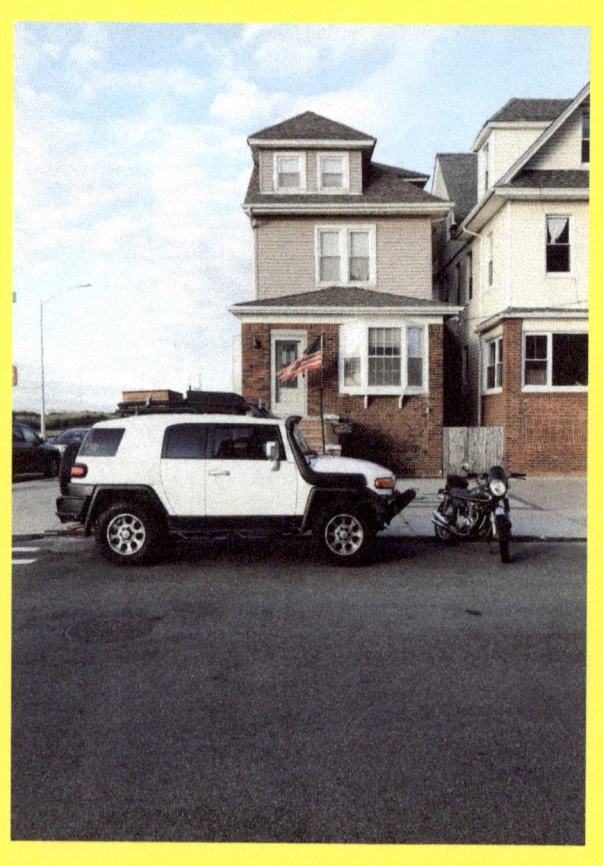

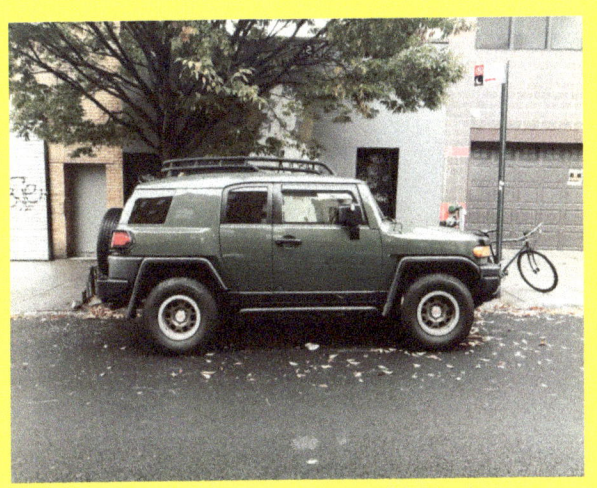

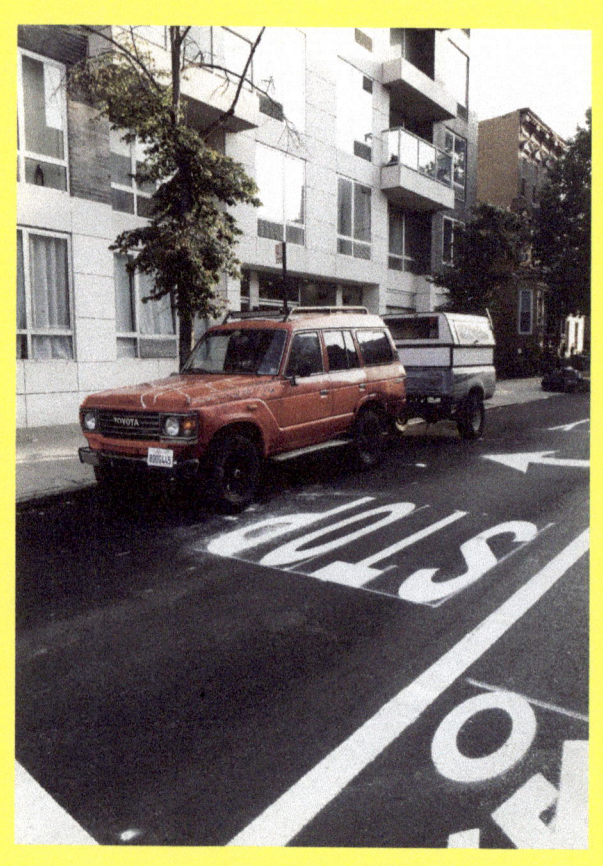

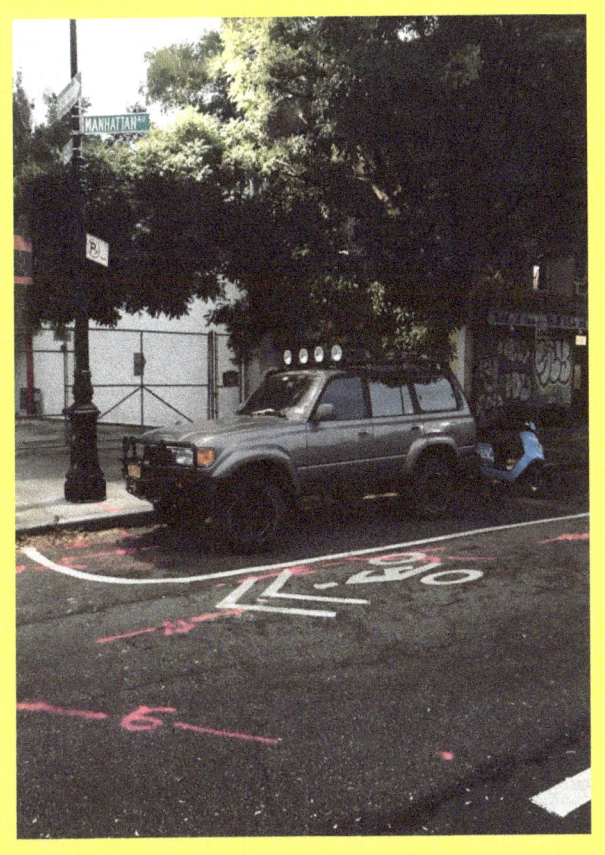

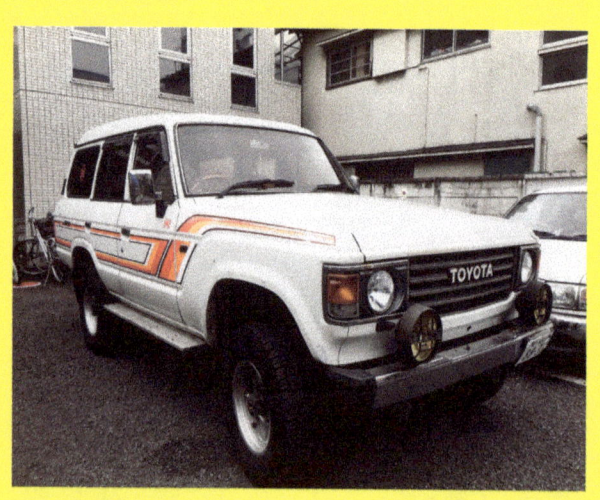

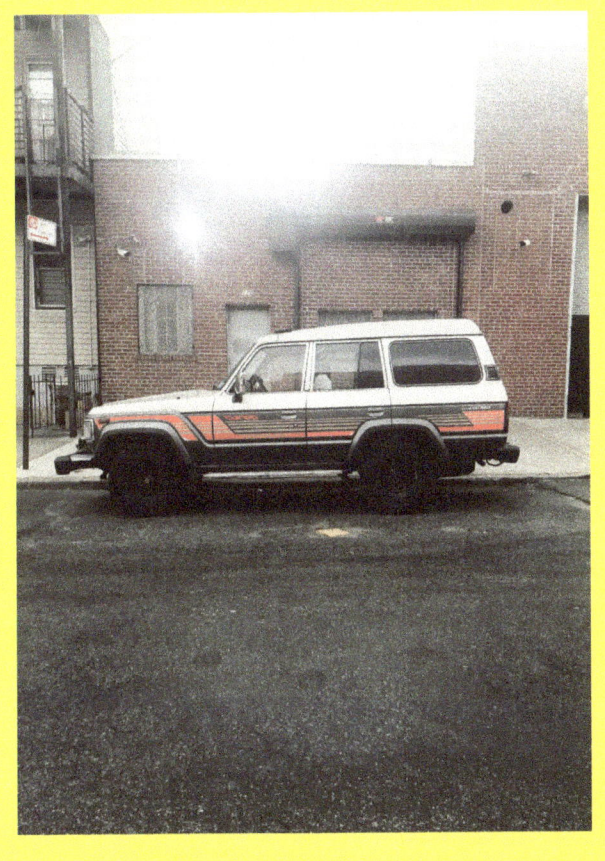

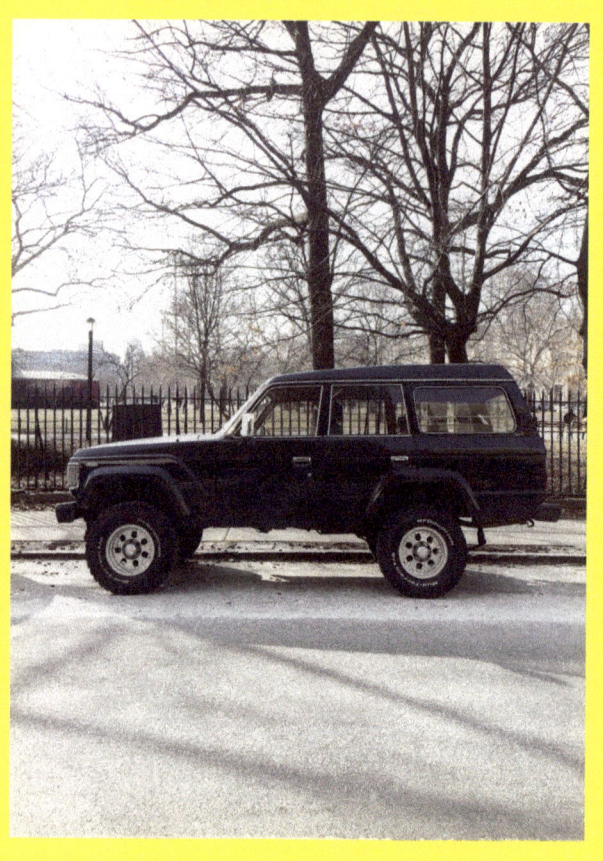

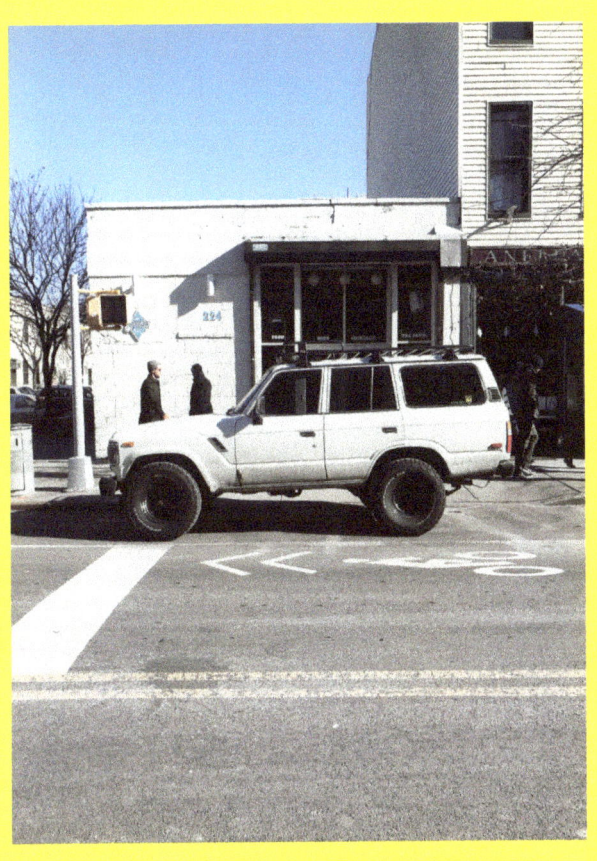

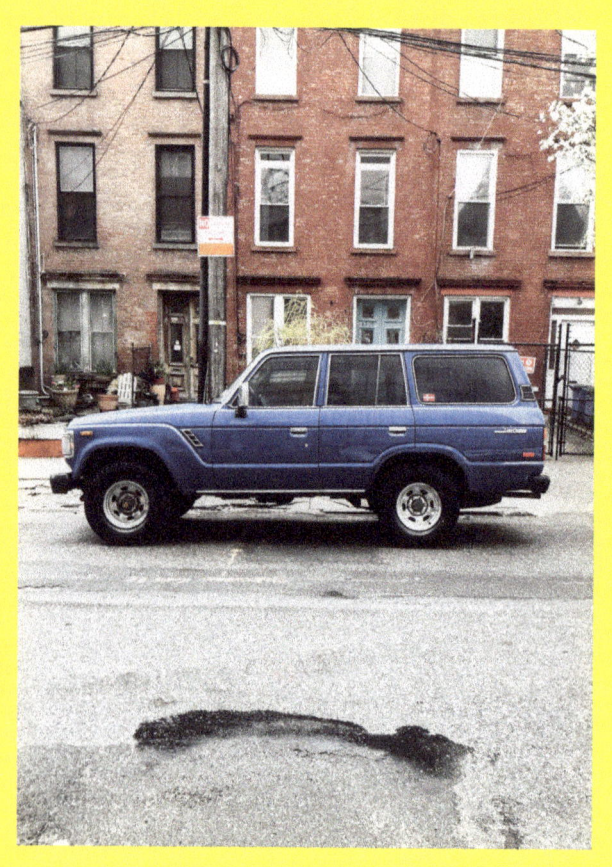

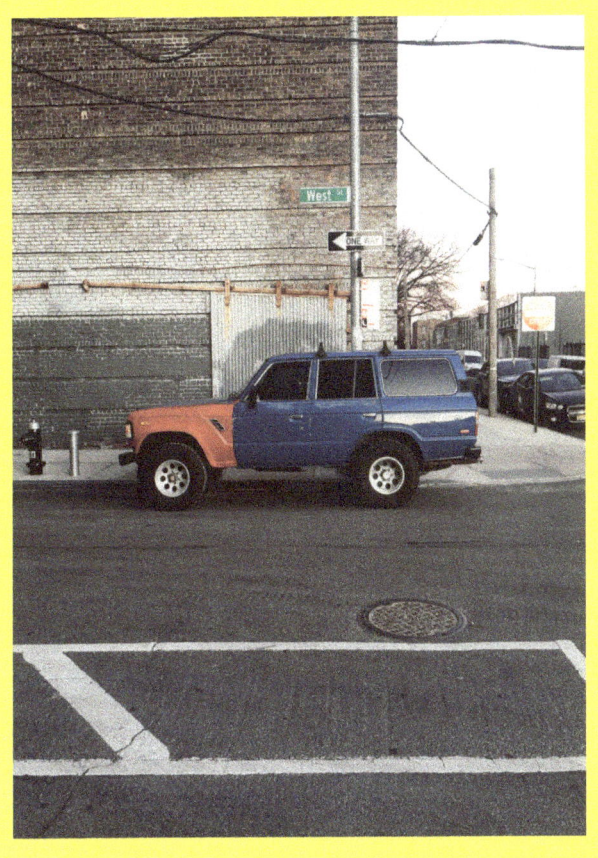

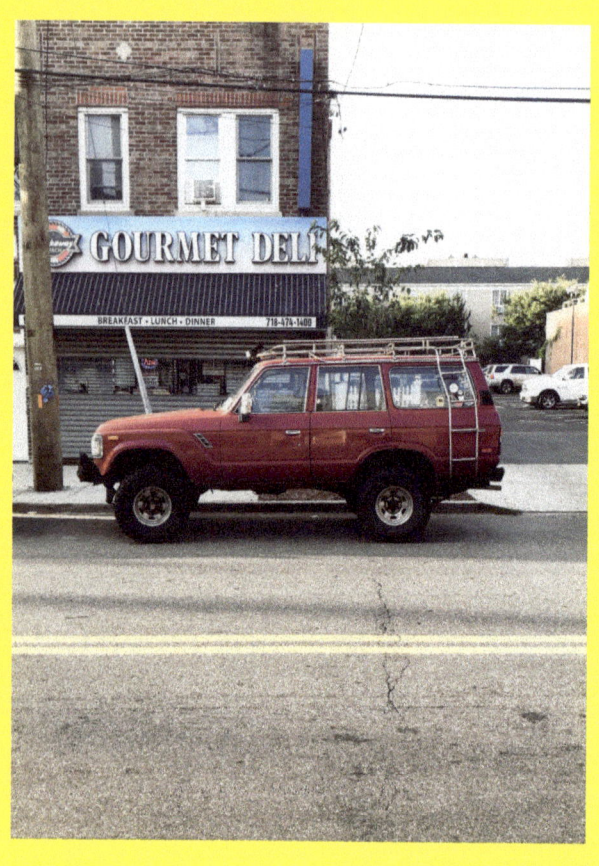

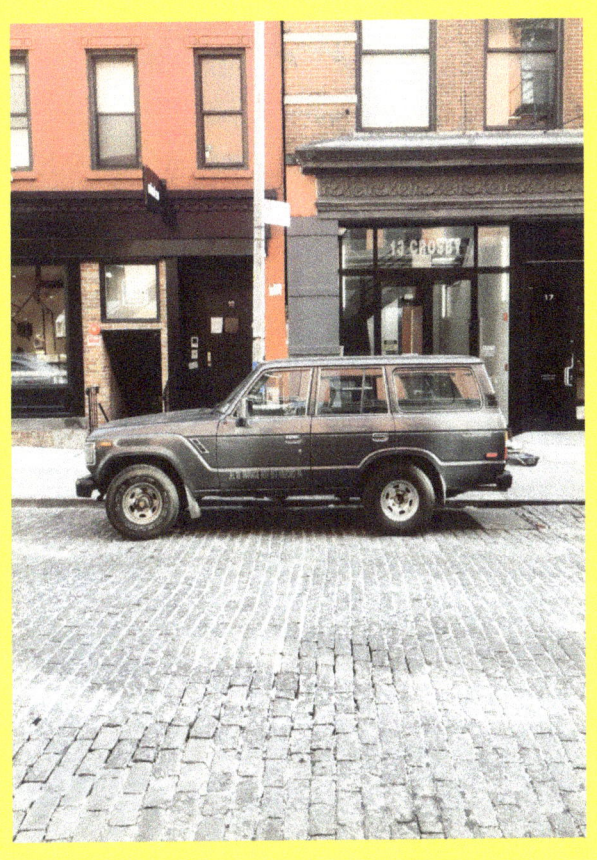

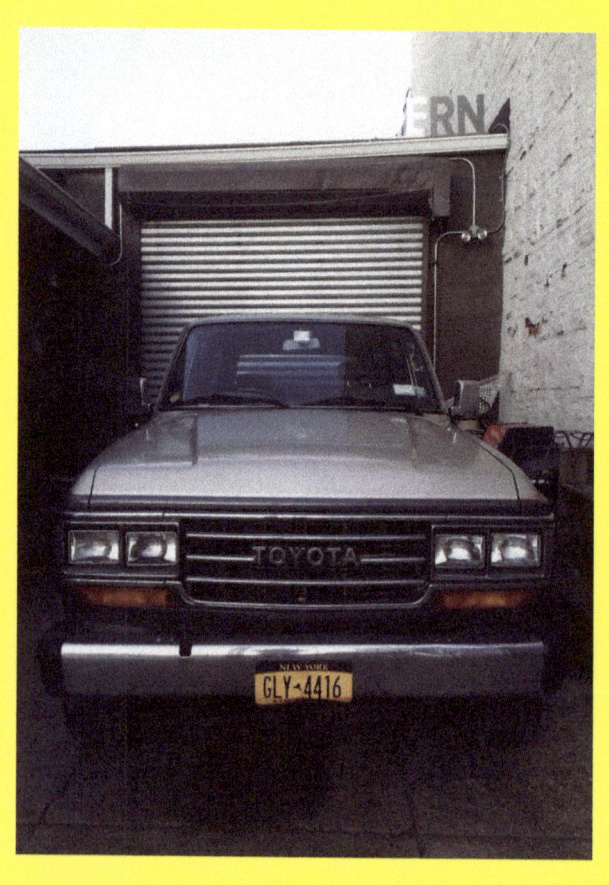

END

END

END

END

END

END

END

END

FAST DON'

FAST DON'T

E FAST DON'T

VE FAST DON'T S

RIVE FAST DON'T STO

DRIVE FAST DON'T STOP

DRIVE FAST DON'T STOP

DRIVE FAST DON'T STOP

DRIVE FAST DON'T STOP

AUTOMOTIVE PHOTO ARCHIVE
BY
MATTHEW JOCELYN

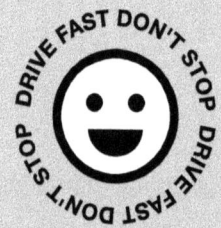

3